A scene from the South Coast Repertory production of *Hold Please.*

HOLD PLEASE

BY ANNIE WEISMAN

DRAMATISTS
PLAY SERVICE
INC.

HOLD PLEASE
Copyright © 2004, Annie Weisman

All Rights Reserved

for my mother

HOLD PLEASE received its world premiere at South Coast Repertory (David Emmes, Producing Artistic Director; Martin Benson, Artistic Director) in Costa Mesa, California, on September 21, 2001. It was directed by Mark Rucker; the set design was by Christopher Acebo; the lighting design was by Geoff Korf; the sound design was by Aram Arslanian; the costume design was by Joyce Kim Lee; and the stage manager was Edward Tighe. The cast was as follows:

ERIKA .... Tessa Auberjonois
AGATHA .... Kimberly K. King
JESSICA .... Jillian Bach
GRACE .... Linda Gehringer

HOLD PLEASE was subsequently produced by Working Theater at Blue Heron Arts Center in New York City, opening on February 25, 2003. It was directed by Connie Grappo; the set design was by James Youmans; the lighting design was by Jack Mehler; the sound design was by Laura Grace Brown; and the costume design was by Ilona Somagyi. The cast was as follows:

ERIKA .... Emma Bowers
AGATHA .... Laura Esterman
JESSICA .... Jeanine Serralles
GRACE .... Kathryn Rossetter

CHARACTERS

ERIKA - *young, affair w/ Solomon*

AGATHA - *married 12 yrs.*

JESSICA - *young, boyfriend*

GRACE - *middle age, had an affair w/ Solomon*

PLACE

An office.

TIME

The present.

- Women are not always protective of other women.

HOLD PLEASE

ACT ONE

Prologue

Loud music. Lights up on four empty office cubicles. Two cubicles are cozily decorated with dried flowers, photos, beanie babies, etc. Two cubicles are unadorned. A phone rings once, then stops with a loud click. Phone rings again, and stops with a loud click. A computer beeps. Another computer beeps. Office lights fade, leaving phone lights and computer monitors clicking, beeping, glowing.

Scene 1

Lights up on the tidy office break room. Jessica, Erika, Agatha and Grace toss a heart-shaped pillow from person to person as they speak. Erika holds the heart.

ERIKA. OK, um, I think —
AGATHA. *(A friendly reminder.)* Uh-uh, feelings only!
ERIKA. Oh. Sorry. I just —
AGATHA. No apologies! Just feelings. And when you're holding the heart, the rest of us have our ears open and our mouths shut.
JESSICA. You don't have the heart. *(Beat.)*
AGATHA. It's OK not to have the heart when you are talking procedure.
GRACE. That's true.

7

AGATHA. Thank you Grace. Otherwise, it's feelings only. *(Beat.)*
ERIKA. OK —
AGATHA. Unless we need to reinforce the rules.
ERIKA. OK, I was … I'm just not sure the feeling. I'm sorry. I just FEEL like I was wrong about him. I didn't really realize.
JESSICA. So … you feel betrayed?
ERIKA. OK.
AGATHA. Jessica, you don't have the heart.
JESSICA. Right … sorry. *(Erika tosses the pillow to Jessica.)* I feel frustrated that some one person's actions could create such a penumbra of unprofessional space. I feel he undermined my self-confidence as a woman at work and I feel he's a detriment to the advancement of our gender. *(She tosses the pillow to Grace. Short pause.)*
GRACE. I feel sorry that he upset you ladies so much.
AGATHA. That's really not a feeling Grace.
GRACE. I'm sorry. I just feel awful that he upset people I consider to be my coworkers and friends. *(Silence. She hands the pillow to Agatha. Agatha closes her eyes. Beat. She opens them.)*
AGATHA. Rage. *(She puts the pillow aside.)* Thank you everyone for your courage and candor. Are there any other feelings? Any feelings? Then let's move on to reporting and recording his actions. Jessica?
JESSICA. I don't have the heart.
AGATHA. We're done with the heart. Now we record his actions to report to the Behavioral Balance committee. *(They pick up their cups of coffee. The younger women use paper cups, the older women use mugs.)* Jessica will serve as our amanuensis. *(She hands Jessica a steno pad and pencil.)*
GRACE. Am I on the Behavioral Balance committee?
AGATHA. You're on the Refrigerator Hygiene committee.
JESSICA. Who's on the Behavioral Balance committee?
AGATHA. A diverse team of company support staff. I'm the chair. Let's get started. First we'll read the confessional cards, and record them under two categories. The grey area of suggestion, and the black-and-white area of outright action. Jessica?
JESSICA. *(Draws out a note.)* OK. "I was walking the narrow hallway from the bathroom to my desk, when Xavier stopped me and said, "Open for business?" I looked down to find my fly was undone. It made me feel completely — "
AGATHA. Uh-uh. We don't need the feeling. That seems pretty clear. One hash mark under action.

ERIKA. I don't know. That sounds more like a suggestion to me.

GRACE. I'd have to agree with that. *(They all look to Jessica. Beat.)*

JESSICA. Yeah, I mean, he didn't DO anything. Per se.

AGATHA. Very well. Next?

JESSICA. *(Draws another card.)* "I was taking his dictation sitting cross-legged in a folding chair I'd brought into his office. He suddenly stopped and asked me if I'd like to move to the couch where he said I'd be more 'comfortable.' Only when I stood up to go did I realize, *(Turns the card over.)* That the couch is so overstuffed you could see straight up the center of my skirt." *(Erika moves to laugh, then covers it.)*

AGATHA. Now that, you'll all agree, is an action.

GRACE. But after all, it is an awfully comfortable couch. *(Beat.)*

AGATHA. He brought that couch from his private home, didn't he? It certainly wasn't ordered from our furniture supplier. There's nothing that overstuffed in their executive collection.

GRACE. Yes, I think he did bring it from home.

AGATHA. There are even some old drink rings on the wooden arms.

GRACE. Those arms are made from the wood of a maple tree that grew in the private grove of his family's mountain home. Vermont maple trees produce a wood that's silky smooth on the surface, and granite hard underneath. I heard him say so.

AGATHA. Why don't we make a note of that?

ERIKA. Those two confessional cards look like they're in the same handwriting.

AGATHA. Why don't we make a note of that too? Let's move on.

GRACE. How many are there?

JESSICA. *(Counting.)* Nine, ten, eleven …

AGATHA. We only need ten for a grievance.

GRACE. Then what?

JESSICA. Then we have a hell of a lot of letterhead to reorder.

ERIKA. He can get fired for this?

GRACE. Honestly, Agatha, what happens to him?

AGATHA. It's out of our hands. We're not the ones making the decisions. We only lubricate the machinery of corporate communication.

ERIKA. Is he gonna know it's us that's ousting him?

AGATHA. That's the beauty of our anonymous reporting system. It's a clarion call from all of us. It's a collective expression of our observations. *(Beat.)*

ERIKA. He's gonna know it's us.

AGATHA. I'd like to say something that might at first sound trivial and personal but is, in fact, not. *(A deep breath.)* I may not have a degree in Business Administration. A private washroom. A burgundy calfskin briefcase. I may have to carry my belongings in an Ovarian Cancer Awareness Month complimentary canvas tote bag and I may work in a cubicle with a partially obstructed view of the loading dock. *(Beat.)* But I still have the right to an Appropriate Professional Environment. We all do. We may have to make a few sacrifices. We may have to do some damage. We may not, at first, be liked. But we must, we MUST, continue. *(Lights shift.)*

Scene 2

The office. Jessica and Erika sit in neighboring cubicles at nearly paperless desks. They wear headsets and sit in swivel chairs. The phone rings by a light flashing, no sound. They type their messages into their computers.

JESSICA. D'ju bone 'im?
ERIKA. No.
JESSICA. D'ju blow 'im?
ERIKA. Yeah.
JESSICA. D'ee go down?
ERIKA. No.
JESSICA. D'ju sleep there?
ERIKA. No.
JESSICA. Ride home?
ERIKA. Yeah.
JESSICA. D'ee call?
ERIKA. No. *(Beat.)*
JESSICA. *(Tallies on her fingers.)* Blow job. Ride home. No call?
ERIKA. Yeah. *(Beat.)*
JESSICA. I win.
ERIKA. How come?
JESSICA. Got a page. At eight.
ERIKA. A page is not a call. It's more like a yank on a leash.
JESSICA. A page says something. No call says nothing. I win.
ERIKA. But at eight?

JESSICA. Eight's before nine!

ERIKA. Barely. *(Phone light flashes.)*

JESSICA. What's an amanuensis? *(Erika shrugs in response. Jessica answers, phone voice.) SolomonXavierGreenspanSachs. No he's not d'you want his voicemail. Thank you.*

ERIKA. You still say Xavier.

JESSICA. I know. Habit. I can't stop saying it. *(Beat.)* You know he's the one who made sure his name came after Solomon's. He wanted SX first in the firm name. You know, SX.

ERIKA. No.

JESSICA. Like they do on all the newer model sports cars with the bigger engines. You know what they're always advertising! S. E. —

ERIKA. X! Oh!

JESSICA. *SolomonXavierGreenspanSachs.*

ERIKA. I get it.

JESSICA. *No he's not d'you want his voicemail. Expect him any minute. Will do, thanks.*

ERIKA. *SolomonGreenspanSachs. It's 111119 N. Hydrangea Boulevard Fourteenth Floor. Thank YOU.* You're still saying it!

JESSICA. *SolomonXavierGreenspanSachs.* I know! Damn it! *No he's not d'you want his voicemail. No, I do not. I can take down a message and have him call you. (Beat.) No, I'm afraid I do not. (Beat.) No, I can't. (Beat.) No, I'm sorry. (Beat.) No. (Beat.) Uh-uh. (Beat.) Yes, I will! Thanks!*

ERIKA. Just tell yourself no more. You won't say it anymore. *(Types something into the computer.)* Amanuensis. The compusaurus says it means scribe, note-taker, secretary. *(Phone flash.)* You.

JESSICA. *SolomonXavierGreenspanSachs.* Shit. *No he's not d'you want his voicemail.*

ERIKA. It also means "apprentice."

JESSICA. *No, I'm sorry I don't know that. No, I don't think so. No, sir, I don't … well we expect him any minute. I can let him know.*

ERIKA. Apprentice has the word "archaic" next to it though. *SolomonGreenspanSachs. (Jessica shoots her an envious look, Erika shrugs benignly.) No I'm sorry I can't. C'I take a message and have him get back to you? Will do thanks.*

JESSICA. Did you know Xavier is of Mexican extraction? The proper pronunciation is in fact "Havier." Agatha said that one time he walked up and whispered in her ear, "SIN is WITHOUT to Mexicans." And one time, she said he came up and told her to "BALL his rubberbands." And Grace told me that one time he said he'd like her to "REPRODUCE his memos."

ERIKA. I told you that.

JESSICA. Oh. I knew I heard it somewhere. *(Hits one key rapidly.)* YES!

ERIKA. *SolomonGreenspanSachs.* What?

JESSICA. I just scored two hundred fifty thousand on "Spelunk!"

ERIKA. *Hello?* Fine, hang up.

JESSICA. Fifty thousand more and I beat your high score!

ERIKA. Good job. Breaking two hundred is tough.

JESSICA. I know! FINALLY I beat that cocky gay guy in PR! He thinks he's so hot shit just cuz he cultivates all those ferns on his desk with zero natural light. *(Phone flash.)* SolomonXavier Greenspan-Sachs. Fuck. *Yes, I'm sorry Mr. Solomon it's hard to break the habit. Yes. three calls. No, I don't think so. No, I'm not sure. Well a few went straight through to your voicemail, so … Will do, thanks.* Would a thank-you KILL that fucker?

ERIKA. Solomon?

JESSICA. Yeah.

ERIKA. He's on his way in. *(Beat.)* What was his name? Who?

JESSICA. The guy!

ERIKA. Oh. Jai Sun. *(Pronounced Jason.)*

JESSICA. Jason what?

ERIKA. Just Jai Sun.

JESSICA. You don't know his whole name? Whore! *SolomonXavier-GreenspanSachs.* Shit, I'm still doing it!

ERIKA. That IS his whole name. Jai. Sun. He's Korean.

JESSICA. *No he's not d'you want his voicemail.* Korean? *No I'm sorry I don't.*

ERIKA. *SolomonGreenspanSachs.* Yeah.

JESSICA. *Will do, thanks.* Whatsee do?

ERIKA. *No he's not c'I take a message.* Analyst.

JESSICA. For?

ERIKA. *Will do, thanks.* Merck.

JESSICA. Exec?

ERIKA. Yeah.

JESSICA. Senior-level?

ERIKA. No.

JESSICA. Junior-level?

ERIKA. Mid. *(Beat.)*

JESSICA. Goin' out with him again?

ERIKA. Haven't decided. *(Computer beeps. Erika types.)*

JESSICA. *SolomonXavierGreenspanSachs. (A silent victory gesture to Erika, then suddenly hostile.) Yeah! No! Working!* It's Jonathan. *No! Maybe! (Phone flash.) You have to hold please. SolomonGreenspanSachs. Yes! No he's not d'you want his voicemail. Will do, thanks. (Back to Jonathan.) Sweetie, sorry, have to have you hold.* God! He thinks he's a badass just cuz he has a Sioux Warrior tattooed on the skin of his head. Big Fucking Deal! You can't see it unless he shaves his head, which he's done ONCE. Besides, Sioux? I'm sure. He's from Sherman Oaks! *Jonathan? Sorry, but you're gonna have to hold. (Phone flash.) Solomon-GreenspanSachs. No I'm sorry he's not c'I send you to his voicemail. Will do, thanks. (To Erika, sotto.)* You know the muscle? The one you can hold onto, if you want to, inside? I am constantly flexing mine under my desk. It's getting very strong. *Hi, sorry 'bout that. (Beat.) Hello? Jonathan? Are you there? (Beat.) HELLO? (Beat.)* I can't believe it. HE put ME on hold! *(Beat.)*

ERIKA. Wow.

JESSICA. What?

ERIKA. Just broke it off with him. I'm sorry, were you talking to me?

JESSICA. Broke it off with who?

ERIKA. Jai Sun. He just IM's do I want to go out tonight and I IM I can't and he IM's tomorrow night and I IM I can't and he IM'S FINE and I IM FINE, log off and log back on under my pseudonym.

JESSICA. What a prick!

ERIKA. It's guys our age. They're just … young.

JESSICA. Tell me about it.

ERIKA. And they say girls get all gaga after sex? Please. *(Beat.)* They're immature. I'm over it.

JESSICA. Yeah, um, I was telling you something.

ERIKA. Oh. I'm sorry.

JESSICA. No. It's cool. It's just that Jonathan, he — *HELLO? Well yes, I'm here now, but I haven't been sitting here holding for you. I have a very full plate. I'm not a SECRETARY, I'm an ASSISTANT. There IS a difference and it's called GROWTH OPPORTUNITY and you know what, I'm sorry, but I have to have you hold! (Beat. She takes off her headset. Stands.)* Will you watch my phone? I feel dizzy. I'm hypoglycemic. If I don't eat something I'm gonna faint. Besides, I want to see how long I can make him hold.

ERIKA. *SolomonGreenspanSachs.* What's that? *No he's not c'I take a message.*

13

JESSICA. Hypoglycemia is a disease. It can strike anyone. Cover me?

ERIKA. *Will do, thanks.* Sure.

JESSICA. Agatha keeps Nutter Butters behind the microwave. Want one?

ERIKA. What if she notices?

JESSICA. You're not supposed to hide things behind appliances. There are rats in the building you know. Rats. A female rat once waddled behind the copy machine and gave birth to eight offspring. They were wriggling out for weeks. Two of them never made it and they smoldered under the toner cartridge. It took months for the smell to dissipate. It was like … Cambodian. *(Beat.)* Even if she notices, how would she know it's me?

ERIKA. She seems to just, know things.

JESSICA. Well she's a very strong lady. She stood up to Xavier. He won't be staring at our asses any more.

ERIKA. He stared at our asses? *SolomonGreenspansSachs.* There, it's catching on! *No he's not c'I take a message.*

JESSICA. That's what someone said.

ERIKA. *Will do, thanks.*

JESSICA. On this note that Agatha found there was all this talk of how he'd been staring at this employee's ass and doing all these nasty things to her.

ERIKA. She found a note from Xavier?

JESSICA. Yep. On the back of a supply order sheet.

ERIKA. How did she know it was Xavier?

JESSICA. It was signed XXX.

ERIKA. That's how she knew?

JESSICA. Yeah, well that's a non-thinker. X? Xavier? XXX?

ERIKA. Right. Totally. Did she give the note to the committee?

JESSICA. Yeah, I'm sure.

ERIKA. Did he deny it? Did he campaign?

JESSICA. I'm sure. Why do you care! He deserves it. Besides, this company offers the most luxurious severance package in the industry.

ERIKA. No. Dismissal on these grounds means losing all termination compensation. And I heard that Xavier's wife has Stage Four Metastatic Terminal Uterine Cancer.

JESSICA. Wow. Karma!

ERIKA. Yes! Three hundred fifty thousand!

JESSICA. Bitch. I have to take my ten. If I don't eat a Nutter Butter now, I am gonna pass out cold. *(Beat. She looks at the blinking phone light.)* Look at that tiny little blinking plastic pinprick.

I'll show him how to hold. *(Jessica exits. A quiet beat. Erika takes off her headset, picks up the phone, dials, puts her feet up.)*
ERIKA. *Hiya. How's the boss today? No, I'm not. No. They're all gone. They're on breaks. (Phone rings.) No, machine'll get it. Cuz you know what? I'm a really bad secretary. I've been sneaking into your office late at night. I take my tight little shoes off and run my blood-red toenails through the clean white carpet. I straddle your swivel chair, and I rub myself up against your lumbar support until I just can't stand it anymore. (Beat.) I even crack open the box where you keep your Mont Blanc fountain pen, and I pull it out of the velvet sheath and slide it right down the front of my panties. (Beat.) Pink lace. G-string. (Beat.) Yeah, it's really comfortable actually. (Beat.) No, only the cheap kind are scratchy, mine are triple-stitched. There's an empty office now. We could have it all to ourselves after seven-thirty. That's when Janitorial finishes vacuuming Executive. (Pause.) They're putting the cameras in the support staff bays, not in the executive suites. We'll be fine. (Beat.) Unless, of course ... I decide to tell on you. Hand in one of your "order forms" with the special code — XXX. (She laughs.) I'm not kidding. I'm just laughing. (Beat.) But I'm not actually joking around. (Lights shift.)*

Scene 3

Agatha and Grace in swivel chairs without headsets. When the phone rings, they have to pick it up. Agatha types on a typewriter. Makes a mistake.

AGATHA. Darn it on the seam! *(Pulls out correction tape.)* I know Information Services keeps telling us, "Use the online contracts, just pull 'em down off the Internet and off you go." But I tell you I just don't trust it for a second unless I put it right onto the page myself. Now I use the computer of course, for everything else, but, CONTRACTS, LEGAL MATTERS, these I type right onto the original forms. *(She loads and locks the typewriter.)* There's nothing like the feeling of imprinting on something. Especially in triplicate. *(Phone rings.)*
GRACE. Excuse me. *Good morning Solomon Greenspan Sachs may I help you? No I'm sorry he's not in yet may I take down a message and*

have him get right back to you? No, I'm sorry I don't know when that start date will be, but I can take a message and have him get back to you with that! No, I'm sorry I do not. No, I'm afraid I don't know too much about that either. I can leave him a message. I sure will. Thank you. Agatha, is that a new lipstick?

AGATHA.   Yes. They call it Petal.

GRACE.   I thought so. It's just lovely on you, for daytime. It's perfect for your coloring.

AGATHA.   My daughter sent it. She says I'm supposed to be a Spring.

GRACE.   And I'm supposed to be a Winter. I'm supposed to stick with the blue undertones and the silver jewelry.

AGATHA.   But you wear gold don't you?

GRACE.   No no no, never! Gold around my face makes my teeth look yellow and my eyes look gray and lifeless. That's what my sister-in-law says anyway, and she's a corporate gift shopper.

AGATHA.   You won't believe what else my daughter sent me. Lip gloss. Can you imagine! At my age?

GRACE.   They're showing it again. In all the magazines.

AGATHA.   Well I tried a little on and I tell you I looked like I just got roughed up by a loan shark. Like I had two fat lips. *(Grace laughs.)* I'm too old for that kind of emphasis.

GRACE.   Besides, we did that in the seventies, the first time around. Remember? *(Grace laughs. Phone rings.)*

AGATHA.   I remember.

GRACE.   Excuse me. *Good morning Solomon Greenspan Sachs, may I help you? No I'm sorry he's not in the office just yet, but may I take down a message and have him call you back? I'm not sure yet. Can I take a message and have him call you right back? Thank you very much. (Not aware she's doing it, she sings under her breath.)* "That's the way the way, uh-huh uh-huh, I like it, uh-huh uh-huh … "

AGATHA.   Do you smell that? *(Phone rings.)* Excuse me. *Good morning Solomon Greenspan Sachs, may I help you? No I'm sorry he's not just yet may I take a message? I'm gonna have to ask him when he gets in. No, I don't have the answer to that. No, I'm sorry. I am going to have to have him call you when he gets back. Thanks so much.* Someone flagrantly over-microwaved their popcorn again. I posted what I thought was a very threatening sign.

GRACE.   You posted that anonymous warning?

AGATHA.   Yes. I thought I might serve as the conscience for a generation that seems to have lost theirs.

GRACE. *(Singing under her breath.)* "That's the way, uh-huh uh-huh, I like it, uh-huh uh-huh." How did that get in my head? Excuse me. *Good morning Solomon Greenspan Sachs may I help you? No I'm sorry he's not in yet may I take down a message and have him get right back to you? Thank you.* Agatha, what is that you're typing?

AGATHA. Employment Termination notice. Mr. Joaquin Xavier. Reason. Sexual Harassment. *(A loud alarm sounds. A single blast.)*

GRACE. I don't think it is popcorn. I think something else is being burned.

AGATHA. What?

GRACE. Maybe it's a toner scorch. The fax in junior executive does that when it's allowed to dip below the advised level.

AGATHA. Doesn't a warning bell go off?

GRACE. Not always.

AGATHA. A warning bell HAS to go off.

GRACE. Not always.

AGATHA. Well surely there's some warning system in place.

GRACE. There's supposed to be. *(Another loud alarm blast.)* I hope you don't mind me asking, but there's a man I thought I could set you up with.

AGATHA. Oh no. It's not some angry divorcé is it?

GRACE. No, Vincent is a lovely, gentle man. He's a minister. But he's Unitarian, so he's very open. He's also a talented cellist. But surprisingly personable. And he has got Matt Lauer teeth. *(Beat.)*

AGATHA. I do love the plaintive sound of a cello. *(Pause. Alarm blasts again.)*

GRACE. Should we evacuate?

AGATHA. It will turn off.

GRACE. When?

AGATHA. Wait. Just wait. In my experience these alarms pass. *(Alarm does a half-blast, then stops.)* There. I told you. *(Reads a memo on her desk.)* Well, if he isn't — *(Beat. Outraged, to Grace.)* A request from Solomon for four more Mont Blanc pens! Could you choke on the nerve of it! These aren't ballpoints spit out of some sweatshop in Macau! Each one is hand-tooled by a skilled Swiss artisan. *(Loads and locks typewriter.)* I'll process the requisition but I won't go to the mat with supplies management if they red-flag it. Not this time. No sir.

GRACE. *(Sniffs.)* I still smell something burning. *(They both sniff. A pause. They sniff again. A pause.)*

AGATHA. I'm sure he's a very nice man. Your minister. But I

17

think I've been set up enough. I think we all have. And remember, you and I still have a job to do. *(She looks at Grace. A challenge.)*
GRACE. Yes. That's right. *(Grace rises, takes her purse and goes. Lights shift.)*

Scene 4

A small ledge. Big enough for two people to stand on, but still a little dangerous. Wind, street noise. Grace lights Erika's cigarette.

GRACE. I love the smell of cigarette smoke. It makes me think of a fire in the hearth on a Christmas ski trip. Everyone sitting around in colorful turtlenecks and festive sweaters, sharing stories from the day on the slopes.
ERIKA. Do you ski?
GRACE. No.
ERIKA. Well it sounds like you have a close family!
GRACE. Yes, it does. *(Beat. Erika smokes. Grace holds her cigarette, unlit.)*
ERIKA. I think about global warming and how they try to negotiate worldwide treaties to limit greenhouse gas emissions. And they fail. I figure this way — *(Inhales, exhales.)* At least I control it.
GRACE. Sometimes, while I'm smoking a cigarette, I feel as though there were a song playing about me in the background. Like in a movie. *(Beat.)* What a silly thing to admit!
ERIKA. No! I know what you mean. *(Beat.)* Are you gonna light that?
GRACE. Oh I can't. Not right now. I'm just holding it, because you see — *(Looks around.)* I'm pregnant!
ERIKA. Oh. Congratulations!
GRACE. Well, it's not planned, but it'll be welcomed. I'm telling Walter tonight. Between dessert and *Law and Order*.
ERIKA. How far along are you?
GRACE. Just about two months. It's really too early to tell people. You never know. With Shelly we didn't tell anyone until about six months. We just couldn't stand the idea of disappointing people if anything were to go wrong. *(Pause. Erika reaches to touch her belly.)*

ERIKA. Can I?

GRACE. Sure. Uh, go ahead. *(Erika puffs on her cigarette as she touches the belly. A pause.)*

ERIKA. Wow. All the genetic information it takes to make a person in such a small, warm place. *(Beat.)* It's like the Internet. *(Grace wiggles away a bit.)*

GRACE. I'm sure there's not much to feel yet.

ERIKA. No, I thought I felt something.

GRACE. Probably the Lean Cuisine I had for my lunch. Or the Blackberry Crumble muffins Tessa brought in. Or Carla's goodbye cheesecake. Did you try that?

ERIKA. I don't eat cheese.

GRACE. Good for you. I can't resist anything on a graham cracker crust.

ERIKA. They're always bringing food in aren't they? The women around here. Like they're fattening us up for something.

GRACE. I wouldn't say that.

ERIKA. I don't know. People will drink warm urine if you leave it in the break room long enough, I swear it. Anything to get through the day.

GRACE. We all get hungry.

ERIKA. Is it true you can tell if it's a boy or a girl?

GRACE. I don't think so.

ERIKA. They say boys stick out more, and girls kind of hang back?

GRACE. That's an old wives' tale, I'm sure.

ERIKA. I've heard that boys just bang around in there, like their body already belongs to them, even when they're only the size of a silver-dollar pancake. I believe it. *(Beat. Erika takes a deep drag, Grace breathes in the smoke.)*

GRACE. Someone's been telling you half-truths and lies. *(They both exhale. Erika looks at her cigarette.)*

ERIKA. Oh my god! I shouldn't be smoking!

GRACE. No, it's okay. I don't mind. My mother smoked Kool menthols and drank Gin Rickeys through all five of her pregnancies and we all came out with ten fingers and ten toes. *(Beat.)* Well, Jeremy's foot has that webbing, but it's made him an awfully strong swimmer. He got a full ride to Villanova out of that.

ERIKA. I should put it out.

GRACE. No, no. Please. *(Beat.)* This might shock you, but I believe that just about every rule can be broken. That's why they're there! To be broken. Just look at those serving sizes they print on everything nowadays. They tell you to eat SIX corn chips, or HALF an oatmeal cookie. Now come on! Life is hard. We deserve to break the rules.

ERIKA. You know what, that is my belief system. And I didn't realize it until just right now.

GRACE. We're surrounded by people who just take the rules too seriously sometimes.

ERIKA. Too literally. They only see the surface. What looks right or what looks wrong.

GRACE. That's right. Now can I just have one little puff off that. It smells so good!

ERIKA. Well, sure. I mean, go ahead.

GRACE. Thank you. *(Takes a drag, reluctantly blows it out. Takes another quick drag before handing it back.)* Those are very … robust. I can't believe they're Native American Lights!

ERIKA. Actually, these are Marlboro Reds. I just put them in this box, cuz it looks better.

GRACE. You're kidding.

ERIKA. Well it's like you said. We're entitled to a little more.

GRACE. You won't say anything, right?

ERIKA. Of course not.

GRACE. I feel I can trust you somehow. *(Grace reaches for the cigarette, Erika hands it over. Grace looks at it.)* I met my Walter right here at the workplace you know. He was a consultant with us for a few weeks. And one complete gentleman. We still go on dates. We go to that same steakhouse where we had that first dinner date every anniversary. Of course, it changed hands and now it's a chain. It's more of a bar than a restaurant now, and they play loud music, and they have a Karaoke night, and the food is just awful. I mean really unclean. Walter got a violent bout of food poisoning from their Surf and Turf. I thought I'd never get that tartar sauce vomit off my bathroom tile. But still, we go there every year. It's tradition now. *(She takes a big pull on the cigarette, blows it out.)* I've never had a problem with the power of men at the workplace. *(She hands back the cigarette. A pause.)*

ERIKA. How long have you known Agatha?

GRACE. Since I've worked here.

ERIKA. Has she always been …

GRACE. No. It's just since the incident.

ERIKA. What incident?

GRACE. Please don't ask me. I really can't say. She just hasn't been the same since.

ERIKA. Did Xavier ever …

GRACE. Did he ever, what? *(Erika takes a drag, blows it out.)*

ERIKA. I mean, did they get all his stuff out yet?

GRACE. Oh yes. They brought in two hulking Samoan security guards to gather his things and escort him out so he doesn't lift anything sensitive off the database.

ERIKA. I heard his wife is like, dying and he kind of needs to be with her.

GRACE. Dying? Or just, "dying."

ERIKA. Dying. Like of a disease.

GRACE. Oh, I thought you just meant, you know, "dying."

ERIKA. No, I mean like dead. *(Grace rubs her stomach. Erika puffs her cigarette. Pause.)* So it's probably all for the best. For his wife, and their family.

GRACE. Oh, they don't have children. *(By way of explanation.)* I rescheduled a fertility appointment for him once. *(Beat.)* No one told me it had gotten so serious.

ERIKA. Well, let's hope the new guy they get is more, you know — *(Erika takes a drag.)*

GRACE. Professional and respectful. *(Erika blows out the last drag and puts out the cigarette. Grace breathes in the last puff of smoke.)* How many other things can we totally consume just by breathing them in? Smoke is so easy that way. So is my Walter. Easy.

ERIKA. You're so grown up. I don't mean old. It's just that you seem like you know what you mean when you talk. Like you really know.

GRACE. It's because I'm beloved. By my husband. So I don't get so caught up in some of the stuff around here.

ERIKA. That must be it then. *(Their eyes meet.)*

GRACE. But you're so young. You have nothing but time. *(Lights shift.)*

Scene 5

Agatha in the break room, putting Sweet'N Low in her coffee, stirring it in with her own spoon (labeled) into her own mug (labeled). Grace enters.

GRACE. I did my best.

AGATHA. And?

GRACE. I honestly got nothing from her.

AGATHA. Nothing?

GRACE. Not a thing.

AGATHA. She didn't bite.

GRACE. Or she's completely innocent.

AGATHA. Or you kid-gloved the girl!

GRACE. Look. Xavier is gone. And I think it's time to move on. I'm not sure we need to pursue this issue any further.

AGATHA. A wound has been opened. We can't leave it gaping and vulnerable to infection. We need to excise ALL the damaged tissue, before the wound can safely heal. *(Beat.)*

GRACE. Have you been watching cable television?

AGATHA. Chinese takeout and the surgery channel is my new Tuesday night. *(Beat.)* What exactly did you say?

GRACE. Exactly what we agreed on. She didn't seem to care.

AGATHA. These girls have no feelings. It's scary, really. I just know that girl is hiding something. She keeps chewable mint-flavored pre-natal vitamins in an Altoid tin in the top drawer of her desk. I saw her making a refill. It's downright spooky. *(Pause.)* Isn't it?

GRACE. A lot of women use prenatal vitamins. They're very nutrient-rich.

AGATHA. I know there's more to know. Why don't I give it a whirl. I think I can connect with these girls.

GRACE. I'm not so sure. *(Pause.)*

AGATHA. Did I show you the photos of my potential grandson? My daughter is filing adoption papers! I might be a GRANNY! *(She whips out the photo.)*

GRACE. Oh, he's precious!

AGATHA. Look at the cheeks! Could you just eat it for breakfast?

GRACE. Oh, I could just take a bite right there!

AGATHA. When my Lily was two, and the cheeks filled out like that, sometimes I just couldn't stand what a little mushy tushie snuggle muffin she was, I just wanted to EAT HER HEAD! I wanted to grab the head and bite down hard and CHEW AND CHEW AND CHEW!

GRACE. I wanted to eat my daughter's shoulders. They were so soft and shnuggly! I wanted to rip her arms out and eat 'em like short ribs! *(The excitement subsides. Beat.)*

AGATHA. She didn't say anything else?

GRACE. Not a thing. Agatha —

AGATHA. Look at the dimple! Did you see the dimple? *(They continue to look at the photo and make cooing noises. Jessica enters, pours herself some coffee.)*

JESSICA. Is that a baby picture?

AGATHA. It's a flashcard. I'm getting proficient in French. Grace here drills my verbs. *(Agatha conceals the photo.)*

GRACE. *(Checking her watch.)* Look at that! Our tenner's up already! *(A sharp look at Agatha.)*

AGATHA. I'm on my fifteener.

GRACE. I thought you took your fifteener this morning. When you did your tooth-bleaching treatment in the bathroom?

AGATHA. That was my tenner. And it's only a freshening rinse!

GRACE. See how old and forgetful I'm getting! Well I'll see you in a few minutes then. *(Grace exits. Pause. Jessica goes to open the fridge.)*

JESSICA. Is there any milk?

AGATHA. Have you brought any in?

JESSICA. I don't think so.

AGATHA. Then there wouldn't be any for you. *(Jessica holds up a small Tupperware container.)*

JESSICA. Do you know whose this is?

AGATHA. Did you bring it in?

JESSICA. I don't think so.

AGATHA. Then it wouldn't be yours.

JESSICA. It has a label on it. It says "AGATHA." So … it's yours?

AGATHA. It appears to be.

JESSICA. D'you hate if I use?

AGATHA. Be my guest. I only ask that you ask.

JESSICA. *(Pours, tastes, masks disgust.)* What is this?

AGATHA. It's Tuscan Sunset. A cinnamon-scented non-dairy creamer.

JESSICA. Wow. It's very strong.

AGATHA. A little Sweet'N Low lightens it up. *(Agatha offers a packet, but Jessica doesn't accept it.)*
JESSICA. Thank you. *(A tense beat.)*
AGATHA. I have a daughter your age and she too drinks coffee.
JESSICA. You have children?
AGATHA. My Lily's in Orlando.
JESSICA. Oh, Florida.
AGATHA. You've been there?
JESSICA. No.
AGATHA. It's very nice. Her husband works at Sea World. He's an engineer who designs and maintains the ocean mammal tanks. It's very stressful work. VERY political. *(Beat.)* And, oh, the amenities in their condo complex! There is a pool, jacuzzi, sauna, sports court, and a spa staffed by four full-time aestheticians. You can get a complete manicure, pedicure, bikini wax and hair cut with scalp massage for guess how much? Fifty dollars! All of it. They come at you all at once, from all sides, like Pep Boys on a vintage Mustang. *(Beat.)* You have an altogether different sense of personal space in that kind of heat. *(Beat.)* But that's Florida! Nicer. Cheaper. Warmer.
JESSICA. Why don't you move there?
AGATHA. Well it's not that simple. I have my lease on the apartment. My cactus window garden. The rabbits. *(Beat.)* And I have my JOB. I can't just up and leave!
JESSICA. I'm thinking about law school. There's a great program at Florida State.
AGATHA. Is that so?
JESSICA. Yeah, it's fully accredited. You can specialize in sports law, which I have always thought would be both cool and challenging.
AGATHA. Well, have you taken the entrance exams?
JESSICA. Not yet. But I found out about this online prep class.
AGATHA. Those exams are very difficult. You probably need to prepare for them for a couple of rigorous years. You can't just leap into something like the law.
JESSICA.   Well, this online prep class called READY, SET GOALS! says you can be ready to stomp any standardized test in three short weeks. *(Beat. She sits down next to Agatha.)* How long have you worked here?
AGATHA. I got my Sterling Tiffany scarf pin last June. That means twenty-five years. *(Jessica takes this in. A beat.)*
JESSICA. That's a very long time. *(Beat.)* Was Solomon always such an asshole?

AGATHA. He's a busy man. He's under a lot of pressure.

JESSICA. He's a bully!

AGATHA. You don't find him attractive?

JESSICA. SOLOMON?

AGATHA. He's not bad-looking! Strong chin. Broad shoulders. And there's that thin scar above his eye. Like a perfect knife-pleat in a Catholic schoolgirl's uniform.

JESSICA. Um, ew. He's leathery.

AGATHA. Leather is a luxury material to some.

JESSICA. Not to me. *(Pause.)*

AGATHA. Young people get crushes on authority figures. It's a perfectly acceptable phase through which to go. But remember, between a boss and a secretary is an insurmountable asymmetry. That's the part your generation seems to get confused about. You mistake for an opportunity what is really an outright surrender to power. And after all, you girls have choices and opportunities of which we never dared to dream. *(Beat.)*

JESSICA. So I guess you're saying yes. He has been consistent. Asshole-wise. *(Agatha moves closer to Jessica.)*

AGATHA. My first Christmas here, I gave Mr. Solomon a plant. It was an exquisite dwarf palm. And in three weeks it looked like a peach pit. I took it home and tried to rescue it with a little mulch and direct sunlight, and I found this brown residue around the rim of the drainage dish. There was no mistaking the odor. He had been tossing his coffee into the plant every day. Hot coffee in a dwarf palm! *(She almost gets upset, but doesn't.)* Some people have no consideration for the living things of life. *(Long pause.)*

JESSICA. That's why it's so great about the new guy.

AGATHA. There's a new guy?

JESSICA. The new guy replacing Xavier.

AGATHA. I wasn't aware there was a replacement for Xavier yet.

JESSICA. Yep. An exec. Headhunted away from Taylor Traylor and Dane. I have a mole there. *(Beat.)* Isn't it great? We have a new chance! *(Pause.)*

AGATHA. You're not enjoying that creamer are you? *(Jessica shakes her head.)* Can you keep a secret? *(Jessica nods.)* I keep a small container of real half-and-half in a cough syrup jar on the condiment shelf. Some days you just need it.

JESSICA. That sounds nice.

AGATHA. I would be happy to start sharing it with you. *(Lights shift.)*

Tension

25

Scene 6

Erika and Agatha at the computer. Grace at her desk.

ERIKA. So, with THIS button, you hear this line, but they can't hear you. And with THIS one, you hear both lines, but none of them hears you. And when you have your headset on —
AGATHA. No! No thank you. No headset for me.
ERIKA. Oh, you should so try it.
AGATHA. I prefer to hold the phone in my hand, thank you.
ERIKA. But really, the headset simply eliminates neck and wrist strain. Also, I used to get these cramps in my ... well ... ass. *(She points to her ass.)* Holding the phone up was somehow connected to a clenching down there, and I didn't even realize it! *(Beat.)* Plus it leaves your hands free to multitask. *(Beat.)*
AGATHA. I've never had a problem with my "ass." At work or anywhere.
ERIKA. I'm just saying, you don't always know the connections between things. Do you know about reflexology? It says there's a map of your whole self on the sole of your foot. I like the idea of that. I've been researching it online.
AGATHA. While answering the phone, no doubt. *(Beat.)*
ERIKA. You know it's just because they think I'm pretty much the quickest with it, that they asked me to be the one to teach you the new system, that's all. I'm sorry if that insults you or something ...
AGATHA. There's no need to apologize. You've learned this "MASTER" system on a blank slate, whereas Grace and I have seen many a newfangled phone system come and go over the years.
GRACE. Remember the Tele-tron?
AGATHA. Who could forget it?
GRACE. They called it the "eight track tape of the telephone industry." They spent a fortune installing it, and I think it lasted a week.
AGATHA. The seventies were truly an embarrassing decade. *(Agatha turns to Erika.)* Of course YOU probably have a seventies knickknack collection! I just don't see the appeal.
GRACE. My daughter raided my closet for my old crocheted

SHAWLS! Can you imagine? I wouldn't use 'em to line the dog bed. *(Grace and Agatha laugh. It subsides. A beat.)*
ERIKA. I'm more into the sixties than the seventies. A-line dresses. Geometric prints.
AGATHA. Hm. Why don't we move along here. So it's press this to find out the number of the person who's calling, press THIS to phone them back!
ERIKA. You got it! Nice job! See, I knew you could do it. *(Beat.)*
AGATHA. Erika, is it possible for you to teach me this new system without assuming the air of Eunice Kennedy Shriver speaking to a triathlete at the Special Olympics! *(Phone light flashes. A moment about who's going to get it. Agatha does.) Good morning SolomonGreenspanSachs may I help you? No he's not may I take a message and have him get right back to you? Thank you very much.* Oh damn it. I pressed ... oh DAMN it! I pressed the wrong ... Now I don't have the number, oh DAMN it. DAMN it to fiery hell. *Good morning SolomonGreenspanSachs may I help you? No, he's not. Yes I can. You're welcome!* Oh hot fudge sundae, I'll never get it right. Never, never, never. DAMN. *Good morning SolomonGreenspan- Sachs may I help you? Hello? (They hang up.)* OK. There. There I saved the number. It was, that's <u>Solomon</u>'s number, right? And he hung up!
GRACE. When?
AGATHA. Just now.
ERIKA. Oh, you might not have done it right.
AGATHA. I pressed that. And I got that. And if I'm not mistaken, that's Solomon's cell phone number. Does he know I'm learning the MASTER system? You don't think he's calling and checking up on me ...
GRACE. Now why would he bother to do that?
ERIKA. He's probably looking for something and then right when you answer he finds it. You know how they are. *(Beat.)* Like that! Always losing numbers and things.
GRACE. I'm sure there's no way he can know which one of us he's calling. Is there? *(They both look at Erika.)*
ERIKA. No. Why would there be? *(Phone light flashes.)*
GRACE. *Good morning SolomonGreenspanSachs may I help you?* <u>Him again. He hung up on me too.</u>
AGATHA. Does he know what the MASTER system is capable of doing? *(A beeping sound. It's Erika's pager. She picks it up, checks the number. A beat.)*

ERIKA. You know what? I have to go to the bathroom. *(She exits. A pause.)*

AGATHA. Has she always carried a pager?

GRACE. I think that was one of those two-way radios they've been advertising.

AGATHA. Well I've never seen it on her before. *(Silence.)*

GRACE. He's not calling back.

AGATHA. She didn't take her purse with her to the bathroom. And I've noticed that she hasn't taken her purse to the bathroom all week. That might mean she's late.

GRACE. You know her cycle?

AGATHA. We're synchronized. Yours started yesterday, didn't it? *(Beat. Grace nods.)* I just know she's got something to hide. *(Lights shift. Erika on the ledge, alone, talking on a cell phone.)*

ERIKA. *They knew it was you hanging up because I'm teaching them the new phone system. Things'll go a lot smoother around here if we're all on board with it, that's all. (Beat.) No, it's okay, it's just you'll have to only two-way me, and if it's safe I'll pick up, and if it's not, I'll slip away and call. It'll be hot! Cloak and dagger, cell and beeper — (Pause.) So, we won't do it in the office anymore. But we're still going to your lake house for Columbus Day, right? Well I could meet you there if you tell me — (Beat.) Over, as in like, "we're over it," or over as in like OVER. (Beat.) You don't think these women can actually do anything! They're just a bunch of busybody secretaries! (Beat.) So, all the better. Now they'll back off for a while. Besides I heard his wife is dying so he kind of needed be with her anyway — (Beat.) No, that's not what I meant, you think I would say something like that? I'm, I'm not like that — (Beat.) No! Don't call me back. Don't hang up. I'll hold. It's okay! I can hold for you. (A long pause while she holds, waiting for him to come back. He doesn't. Then the street sounds increase as Erika starts to cry. The honking, driving and yelling from below become loud, then deafening. Lights shift.)*

Scene 7

Break room. Jessica at the table. Agatha enters.

AGATHA. Would you like a Nutter Butter? I keep some behind the microwave.

JESSICA. Oh, no thank you.

AGATHA. I think I'll treat myself. It's been a hard day. *(She goes to get the Nutter Butters, they're gone.)* What? You didn't see anyone taking my Nutter Butters, did you?

JESSICA. No.

AGATHA. You think you find a safe place. But you never know.

JESSICA. You keep Nutter Butters in here?

AGATHA. Behind the microwave. I'm hypoglycemic, so I sometimes need a little boost, and I find that Nutter Butters really do the trick.

JESSICA. I'm hypoglycemic too!

AGATHA. So you understand!

JESSICA. Of course. Not that anyone else does. They don't even know what it is.

AGATHA. It's a disease.

JESSICA. But they think we make it up. That it's "emotional." But it's a PHYSICAL FACT.

AGATHA. I'm going to call another heart talk. I think we have some issues to discuss.

JESSICA. Like what?

AGATHA. Food theft for starters. And I'd like to discuss creating a clothing policy. You've done a wonderful job combining a young look with a look that's professional.

JESSICA. Thank you.

AGATHA. But there are other people, like Erika, who lack the self-respect it takes to dress appropriately. It's very hostile, I think — the scooped-neck tops and the visible bra straps. *(Beat.)* And whatever happened to scarves? A scarf is very sophisticated. A scarf says, "I'm a woman, not a porterhouse steak!" *(Beat.)*

JESSICA. I wouldn't have used the word hostile, but now that you mention it ...

29

AGATHA. Well, I'd like to call another heart talk.

JESSICA. We just had one though.

AGATHA. We can use one of our Urgent Issue heart talks. We're allotted two extra a year for circumstances like this. I'm going to need something to eat right now.

JESSICA. I have some pretzels, if you want.

AGATHA. Oh, I feel just awful taking your food.

JESSICA. Don't play the shame game. It's not your fault. Here. *(Gets the pretzels, gives them to Agatha. Agatha eats, relieved.)*

AGATHA. Thank you, you're very kind. *(Beat.)*

JESSICA. I got called a bitch! By my boyfriend. We were fighting and he called me a frigid bitch.

AGATHA. I got called that consistently throughout my twelve-year marriage. *(Beat.)* He used to go away on three-month Navy deployments and I'd be in our Quonset hut trying to re-light the pilot with the Zippo he bought me at the military base — for our wedding anniversary! — so I could make Lily her Chicken 'n Stars. It's a miracle I didn't blow us both to bits. And just once I'd be crabby or short with him and what would he call me? What would he say?

JESSICA. "You fucking bitch." *(Pause.)*

AGATHA. How old is your boyfriend?

JESSICA. My age.

AGATHA. And how old are you, if you don't mind me asking?

JESSICA. Not at all. Twenty-four. *(Beat.)* He won't commit. Not that I really want him to. But he won't.

AGATHA. You don't want him to?

JESSICA. Well I don't know!

AGATHA. He's got somebody else?

JESSICA. Why do you say that?

AGATHA. Well if he won't commit, very often that means, they've got their eye on somebody else. I seem to sense that that's what's going on.

JESSICA. Well I don't know.

AGATHA. Does he call you and say he is "running a little late?"

JESSICA. Yeah, a lot.

AGATHA. That he has to "work late"?

JESSICA. Yeah.

AGATHA. Where does he work?

JESSICA. Taylor, Traylor and Dane. He's in duplication. *(Agatha looks at her quizzically.)* He's the copy boy.

AGATHA. Did you meet him on the job?

JESSICA. Yes. Kind of.

AGATHA. Here?

JESSICA. He used to deliver us stuff from ReproMan, but they offered him an inhouse gig at TTD. Dental, *y todo. (Beat.)* He's half-chicano. *(Beat.)* Neither of us is doing this for life. He's trying to decide if he wants to go into his Dad's business, go bring vaccines to developing nations, or pursue his music.

AGATHA. And you?

JESSICA. Well, I might just go get my teaching credential. And teach. I'd like to teach small children. *(Beat.)* Very small children.

AGATHA. And then there's "sports law."

JESSICA. Oh, yeah. I'm also interested in that.

AGATHA. Well, teaching is very important work.

JESSICA. Yeah. And you'd always have that to fall back on. At least here I can just walk away from the job at the end of the day. I'm not at all emotionally installed here. I have like six search portals at any given time. You really think it means he's cheating on me?

AGATHA. Time for me to head back. I'm only on a fiver, and if we're going to stand by our decision to oust Xavier we need to stick to some rules ourselves!

JESSICA. That's very true. Thanks for reminding me.

AGATHA. I consider it my pleasure. You're one of the ones I believe in.

JESSICA. Thank you for saying that. *(Agatha exits. Jessica takes another Nutter Butter out of her pocket, hesitates a beat, then eats it. Lights shift.)*

Scene 8

The office. The end of the day. The overhead lights are off. In the soft glow of four individual desk lights, Erika is sucking on Jessica's neck. Jessica is gleeful, determined.

JESSICA. Harder.

ERIKA. I can't.

JESSICA. Check it. Purple?

ERIKA. Red.

JESSICA. More.

ERIKA. My mouth hurts.

JESSICA. More.

ERIKA. OK! *(Beat. She sucks again.)*

JESSICA. Suck harder. I can't even feel that.

ERIKA. *(She stops.)* I can't.

JESSICA. How does it look?

ERIKA. *(Looks.)* Really gross!

JESSICA. But purple?

ERIKA. No, it's still red.

JESSICA. Then you better suck harder. *(Erika keeps sucking, much harder. In shadow, someone walks in, silently, moves toward the door to Xavier's old office.)* Oh, okay, ouch, stop. *(She stops.)*

ERIKA. There. It's fucking eggplant. *(The shadowy figure turns on the light in Xavier's office, stands in the threshold, observing Jessica and Erika.)*

JESSICA. Good. Ow. *(Takes out a compact.)* Now I apply the concealer.

ERIKA. Isn't that gonna cover it?

JESSICA. Sweet, naïve Erika. My attempt to hide it will make it all the more real.

ERIKA. You really are smart about some things.

JESSICA. I know. Conceal me. *(Erika does.)* God his balls are battered and fried! *(Jessica takes the compact. Admires the work.)*

ERIKA. What exactly did he do to you anyway?

JESSICA. It's what he didn't do, which is be a fucking man! It's always — "I don't know, Mexican, Thai, Shabu Shabu, whatever!" I'm sick of having the opinions! He's like — *(Beat. Puts down her makeup.)* a puffy down comforter you have to lie under, FREEZING, until your own body heats him up! I'd like a pile heavy woolen blankets pressing me down into bed. I'd like to go to sleep at night with something I can feel myself against! *(Picks up her makeup. Phone light flashes.)* Shit. It's Solomon. You? *(Erika stares at the phone.)* K'you get it?

ERIKA. No.

JESSICA. It's five-fifty-seven.

ERIKA. So. His watch is five fast.

JESSICA. Does he know? *(Beat.)*

ERIKA. Does he know what?

JESSICA. His watch is five fast?

ERIKA. No. He doesn't know how to "work the buttons." His

WIFE gave it to him. I had to set it. He doesn't know shit. *(Beat.)* Did it ever occur to you that Jonathan's maybe just fucking someone else? Someone at the office or something?

JESSICA. What makes you say that?

ERIKA. You just said he won't commit to anything! *(Beat.)*

JESSICA. Agatha wants you to dress more professional.

ERIKA. What do you mean more professional?

JESSICA. Beats me, but she wants to heart talk about it. Just giving you a heads-up.

ERIKA. She said I dress like a slut?

JESSICA. She didn't use the word slut …

ERIKA. Figures. Flat women categorically hate me!

JESSICA. She's not flat. She wears minimizers. In her words, "It's a sad day when we need to use our breasts to pad our productivity in the workplace."

ERIKA. Oh and I "use" my breasts?

JESSICA. Well you DO favor the padded push-up bra, which is a very strong choice for daytime. *(Beat.)*

ERIKA. That reminds me … I've been meaning to give you the 411 on the issue of job security. This company is supposedly on the tank.

JESSICA. Who says?

ERIKA. If they're bringing a new man from TTD, don't you think it means they might be reorganizing?

JESSICA. Maybe. *(Beat.)* Why?

ERIKA. He might be one of those management efficiency consultants. Those guys are trained to skeletonize support staffs like us. Have you thought about that?

JESSICA. Well I've been looking online at law schools. I think it would be great to be an advocate for women's health concerns. I got an email recently stating that the bleach they put in tampons is permeating our mucous membranes and in a few years it could cause a worldwide plague of uterine cancer!

ERIKA. Is that true?

JESSICA. I got it online.

ERIKA. So? Is it true?

JESSICA. I don't know!

ERIKA. There are in the world, certain things that either true or not true, now can you tell me, IS THAT TRUE? *(Pause. Jessica stares in her compact.)*

JESSICA. *(A statement.)* How good is my hickey?

ERIKA. Just how long can we be semipermanent employees? And.

where does it lead?

JESSICA. Why don't you try my new lip gloss? It contains relaxing Lotus Blossom oil.

ERIKA. No. *(Beat. Jessica applies lip gloss, admires herself in the mirror, then turns back to Erika.)*

JESSICA. Want to know my secret? *(She points to her lips.)* Permanent lip liner. It's a tattoo on your lips and it's forever. *(She snaps the compact shut.)* How do I look? *(Stands, twirls.)*

ERIKA. Marked. *(Jessica exits. Shadowy figure watches as Erika turns off all the remaining desk lights, except her own. We now see, in profile, that the shadowy figure is a woman in a business suit. Erika still does not see her. Erika picks up the handset and dials. Hangs up. Waits. Then picks it up again, dials. Leaves a message.)* Yes, hello Mr. Solomon, I apologize to you and Mrs. Solomon if I'm disturbing you at dinner at this hour, but I wanted to let you know that you might have left something at the office. I'm certain it's yours. I don't imagine you'd like me to bring it to your home. Of course, it should still be here when you get back to work tomorrow. But in this office, you never know, do you? I hope you have a nice evening, and again, I am so sorry to disturb you. At home. *(She hangs up. The shadowy woman walks into Xavier's office and shuts the door behind her. Erika jumps up, turns. She stares at the door. Lights fade.)*

End of Act One

34

ACT TWO

Scene 1

Next morning. The office. Overhead fluorescents blaze even brighter than before. Jessica is alone at her desk, with a scarf tied elaborately around her neck, and a black eye.

JESSICA. *SolomonGreenspanSachs. No he's not d'you want his voicemail. No I don't. Nope. No. No. No, I'm sorry. Nope. Will do, thanks. SolomonGreenspanSachs. Hi! A lot better, thanks. Well, it's not pulsing and painful anymore. Now it's starting to tingle. The doctor said that means it's going to heal. I can start putting makeup on it tomorrow he said. It looks like I won't even need antibiotics. (Beat.) What time? (Beat.) OK. Chinese at eight tonight. Whatever you say! (A loud buzz. A sound we haven't heard before.) That was her! Our new boss! He's a she! It's a girl! Her name is Diana. She has this buzzing thing. (Buzz.) Yes, Diana? (Beat.) Yes, there's a refrigerator in the executive break room you're free to use. Or I can put it in the support staff mini-fridge for you if you like. That would be no problem as well. If you'd like, I can show you some menus from which we order. There's a great salad place, okay Thai, and for something fun and different: Persian. They make these skewers? And just as an FYI, Erika, my cubiclemate, keeps a large tin of Altoids in the top drawer of her desk and we're all welcome to use them. (Beat.) Um, Hello? (Buzz.) Yes, Diana? Yes, we have a labeling machine. I'd be happy to bring it right in. It's good that you get your labeling done right away. Did I see on the bio you handed me that you went to Pepperdine? Did you know a guy there by the name of Micah Goranson? Red hair, green eyes, psych major, always wore a pair of Stop Sign Red classic Converse? He went to my high school, so I was just wondering. Hello? (Beat.) Jonathan? I think I have to go. I'll see you tonight my love. (Buzz.) Yes, Diana? Oh, I'll be right in with it. And if you were wondering about my eye. My boyfriend hit me. Hello? Diana? Hello? (Erika enters with purpose, immediately starts clearing her desk.) SolomonGreenspanSachs can I assist you? She's here! No he's not d'you*

35

want his voicemail.
ERIKA. Who?
JESSICA. The new guy! *No I'm sorry I can't.*
ERIKA. You said SHE.
JESSICA. *No I'm sorry I don't.*
ERIKA. She?
JESSICA. *Will do, thanks!* She's a she! The new guy's a girl!
ERIKA. Where is she?
JESSICA. Occupying Xavier's former office. Do we have a labeler?
I need to bring her a labeler. She likes to get everything labeled right
away. *SolomonGreenspanSachs.*
ERIKA. He's a SHE? What happened to YOU?
JESSICA. *Yes she is just a moment.* What are you doing?
ERIKA. I'm quitting. I've decided it's time for me to go and pur-
sue my own goals, and … what happened to your face?
JESSICA. Jonathan. He hit me!
ERIKA. Hit you? Or just like, hit you?
JESSICA. He clocked me in the face! Guess how old she is! *(Buzz.)*
She wants the labeler!
ERIKA. Wow. In the face. How old is she?
JESSICA. Do we have a labeler?!
ERIKA. Yes. Agatha has one mounted beneath her desk.
JESSICA. *(Retrieving labeler.)* You can't quit now! *(Buzz. She exits
into Diana's office. Phone light flashes. Erika reluctantly puts on her
headset and answers.)*
ERIKA. *SolomonGreenspanSachs. No he's not d'you want his voice-
mail. Will do, thanks. SolomonGreenspanSachs. No he's not d'you
want his voicemail. (Jessica pops her head in.)*
JESSICA. Erika, do you know where Xavier stored his binder
clips?
ERIKA. *No I'm sorry I don't.*
JESSICA. Can you look for me?
ERIKA. *No I'm sorry I can't.*
JESSICA. Fine! I'll look myself. *(She enters Diana's office.)*
ERIKA. *Will do, thanks. (Silence for a time. No calls. Erika looks at
Diana's door. The door opens, Jessica comes out laughing, goes to get
something from her desk.)*
JESSICA. She can be really clever. When she says things. And she
uses totally foul language on the phone! She's amazing. And guess
how old she is!
ERIKA. I don't know how old she is. Why does she need binder

clips already?

JESSICA. She's doing some binding! She likes to get things started. She's installing a Pilates machine in her office. She said we could use it. It's strengthening and lengthening. We're all shrinking you know. If we don't fulfill our biological imperative to have babies then all those extra hormones eat away at our bones and make us not only lonely but osteoparotic. We need to start Pilates before it's too late.

ERIKA. How old is she?

JESSICA. Twenty-four years old. Our age. Well, my age. You're twenty-six, right?

ERIKA. I'm twenty-five.

JESSICA. In her senior year undergrad she did a simultaneous MBA and after graduation she worked her way up at TTD to be the youngest female executive in the company's history. She's writing a motivational book. But not for women! She's strongly post-feminist. For people. And not for young people! She's strongly post-ageist. It's for people. People who want to COUNT. *(Puts on her headset.)* SolomonGreenspanSachs this is Jessica. Yes she is can I ask you to hold one moment please. Thank you. Diana? Oh, okay, I'll let him know. OK. OK. I can do that. Uh-huh. Yes, no problem. Hello, thank you for holding. I'm afraid she's on an international conference call, but she has asked me to get the information from you. Uh huh. Uh huh. Uh huh. Of course we can handle that. Yep. Yes. Uh huh. Yes, I can. Yes, I will. Uh huh. Have a good one. *(Erika stares at her, incredulous.)* She wanted me to get the information for her. *(Beat.)* She says she wants me to help her out with this special project too. You're not really gonna leave!

ERIKA. I just don't know if I can be here anymore. Something's changed in me. *(Beat.)* He HIT you?

JESSICA. Yeah, well first I met him at the bar and he saw the hickeys right away and of course he freaked and left. Or at least I thought he left, but really he went outside to sulk and smoke one of his French filterless cigarettes. So, out walks CAMUS, and up walks this cutie named Stephen. He's a hip hop artist. He's white. He starts rapping some of his shit for me. It's really fucking subversive. He's like a combination of Eminem and David Mamet. I couldn't hear that well in the club but he gave me one of his CDs. He has CDs.

ERIKA. So. He has a CD burner.

JESSICA. And he has a web site.

ERIKA. So, he has time on his hands. Does he have a record label?

JESSICA. I don't know! Anyway, I'm with Stephen at the bar and he's buying me Amstel Lights and I'm laughing really hard and he's doing this DEAD ON Jim-Carrey-doing-James-Dean impression, it's just DEAD ON. And Jonathan comes charging in and he gives Stephen one hard shove in the chest — like a basketball pass — and then he turns around to walk away, but of course he's wearing his backpack-made-of-retired-vanity-license-plates, which swings around and clobbers me in the face. And Jonathan was so mortified that he grabbed Stephen's margarita on the rocks and clutched the ice cubes right up against my eye. *(Beat.)* The tequila and salt kinda stung really bad, but it was still romantic as fuck. Anyway, we're back together.

ERIKA. What about Stephen?

JESSICA. Do you want me to set you up with him? I got his email.

ERIKA. No thank you. What project are you helping her with?

JESSICA. It's just this efficiency program she's initiating. We're having a meeting about it between shifts today. I'm assisting her on the project. *(Buzz.)* Oh, that's her again sorry. She just keeps needing me.

ERIKA. I guess so.

JESSICA. You better not leave. Besides. You don't have anywhere to go! *(Jessica goes into Diana's office. Pause. Erika notices the different light. Phone rings. She puts on her headset.)*

ERIKA. *SolomonGreenspanSachs. Hello. Well, I just had something to tell you. It was a courtesy call. I wanted to tell you that the new guy's here. And he's a she. Her name is Diana. Well did you know how old she is! Guess! Guess! Guess or I'll tell her what you did to me on her coffee table! Nope. Younger. Younger. Younger. TWENTY-FOUR! Umhm. That's right. I was just giving you the heads-up. Oh and there's something else. I'm pregnant. Positively. I peed on the stick and it came out pink. Today's over-the-counter tests are laser accurate. (Buzz.)* That's Diana. She has a buzzing system. We're all responding very well to it. I have to go. *(Jessica pokes her head in.)*

JESSICA. I'm sorry, are you on the phone?

ERIKA. *No, I'm not.*

JESSICA. Diana wants you to join us in here. D'you mind dialing out?

ERIKA. *I don't have to and I might not want to.*

JESSICA. Erika? Can you dump that call and join us?

ERIKA. *Maybe I won't get rid of it. Maybe I'll hold on to it, because*

I want to. (She hangs up. Jessica goes back into the office. Erika gets nauseous, throws up into a trash can. Buzz. Another wave of nausea. She fights it, takes out her Altoids tin, chews a bunch of them. A double buzz. This time, she answers.) I'll be right in. *(Erika enters Diana's office. Lights shift.)*

Scene 2

Break room. Erika, Jessica, Agatha, Grace sitting as if at a heart talk. The heart is nowhere in sight.

AGATHA. A girl?
GRACE. A woman?
JESSICA. You should see what she is wearing. It's a double-breasted suit jacket with side vents — a nod to the eighties power suit — but she softens it with a simple black skirt to the knee. She has this pin on, and normally I'm not into pins. They're so, you know ...
ERIKA. Auxiliary Luncheon.
JESSICA. Yes. But this one just works. And her body ... unbelievable. I swear to you her ass is half the size of her head. *(Beat.)*
GRACE. Is there something wrong with wearing pins?
AGATHA. What does she go by?
JESSICA. Diana.
AGATHA. What did you call her?
JESSICA. Diana.
AGATHA. Is that how she introduced herself?
JESSICA. Yeah. As Diana. And she said things are going to be different from now on.
AGATHA. I see. *(Pause.)*
GRACE. Did she say why she came so early?
JESSICA. Maybe she wanted to unpack her stuff. Get settled.
ERIKA. And maybe she wanted to look around before any of us got here.
AGATHA. You didn't tell her about the heart talks? *(Beat.)*
JESSICA. No.
AGATHA. Because I would prefer to explain the acronym to her first.

ERIKA. It's an acronym?

JESSICA. What did you think it was?

ERIKA. What does it stand for?

GRACE. No one told me at first, either.

ERIKA. What does it stand for?

AGATHA. Helpful Exercises Afforded to Reception Technicians. It was developed at a national clerical convention in Houston, Texas. I had the honor of representing us there.

JESSICA. Guess how old she is!

AGATHA. How do you know how old she is?

JESSICA. I asked her. You'll never guess how old she is!

GRACE. Fifty.

JESSICA. Younger!

GRACE. Forty.

JESSICA. Younger!

AGATHA. That was awfully impolite of you. You don't just ask a woman her age.

GRACE. Thirty-five?

JESSICA. Younger!

AGATHA. Younger than thirty-five?

JESSICA. Yep. Younger!

GRACE. Thirty-three?

JESSICA. Younger!

GRACE. Thirty-two?

JESSICA. Younger!

GRACE. Thirty-one?

ERIKA. TWENTY-FOUR! She's twenty-four years old, OK?

JESSICA. She has a BA and an MBA and she is the youngest female executive in the history of the company! And she's tougher than shit. I called my phone friend at TTD, she hears everything, and she said one time, Diana put a binder clip on her nipple in a regional meeting, just to scare the shit out of everybody. She left it dangling there while she talked, just to freak everybody out. But she can also be gentle and nurturing. *(Beat.)*

GRACE. Did I miss something? Are pins not "in"? Why, suddenly, are you in a scarf! And what, may I ask happened to your face!

JESSICA. My boyfriend battered me in a jealous rage. *(A loud buzz. Jessica shoots up, picks up a phone.)* Yes of course there's coffee. Let me guess. Cream, no sugar? I can always tell how a person takes it. It's a gift I have. I'll bring you some right away. *(Hangs up.)* Does anyone happen to know if there's any real half-and-half in the fridge? *(A moment between Agatha and Jessica.)*

AGATHA. Why yes. I think there is some. I'll get it. *(Agatha gets the half-and-half for her.)*

JESSICA. She has this project she says will affect ALL of us! She's already asked me to help her out with it. Excuse me, ladies. *(Jessica exits with coffee.)*

GRACE. I didn't know that phone worked. And what project is she talking about?

ERIKA. There's real half-and-half in here? What are you, hoarding it?

AGATHA. I'm not HOARDING anything.

ERIKA. Well you're holding back! Hiding things!

AGATHA. I have nothing to hide. If I've brought in real half-and-half, I have no obligation to make it known. I would have shared it at any time. I only ask that you ask.

GRACE. Agatha, do you know what this meeting is about?

AGATHA. I can only assume it's what we've been waiting for. I told you ladies we were on the right track. We're creating a Purely Professional Environment. I for one, can't wait to hear what she has to say!

GRACE. Agatha. Half-and-half is not a good choice at our age. If the coffee in here is too strong for you, you can add hot water. And there's always tea. We have cinnamon and orange pekoe. And green tea. Green tea is very heart-healthy.

ERIKA. Well I have something to say. You might not want to hear it, but I have something to say! *(Jessica hurries back in, memo in hand.)*

JESSICA. Wow she works fast! She's asked me to read this memo aloud. It's for all of us.

GRACE. Erika just told us she has something to say. Perhaps we should let her say it. *(Beat.)*

JESSICA. Erika. She gave me this memo to read. I think we can put our personal problems aside for a minute and hear it. *(Beat. They settle in to listen.)* "I want to thank you all in advance for your time and attention. As you may know, there are going to be some changes around here. For starters, Solomon, Sachs, and Greenspan are away on a week-long sensitivity-training golf retreat in Palm Desert. In the interim, I have been asked to run an efficiency assessment in my time here. I will be conducting an experiment designed to determine which work models work the best. It's about communication. And it's about time." *(Beat.)* Oh my god a double entendre! Like, "it's about time!" Is there no LIMIT to her gifts?

(No response. She continues.) "You will be the first support staff in the company to benefit from this new testing protocol. The top performer in your division will receive a royal blue ribbon lapel pin, an increase in clerical responsibilities, and a full day of pampering at Henderson's Dude Ranch and Day Spa. *(Beat.)*

ERIKA. What happens to everyone else?

JESSICA. It doesn't say.

GRACE. I'm sure everyone else will be handled fairly.

ERIKA. What makes you sure of that? *(Pause.)*

JESSICA. Well I for one am psyched. This is just what we've been waiting for! *(Lights shift.)*

Scene 3

Loud music. Industrial sounds. The office setup changes shape. Jessica, Erika, Agatha and Grace sit at their desks. Jessica and Erika put on headsets. Agatha picks up her headset. A long beat. Grace puts on a headset. Agatha shoots her a look. Betrayal. A cheerful buzzer goes off. The lights change. The contest begins. The women type and press buttons while music plays underneath them. Cheerful buzzer sounds again, ending the contest. Lights back to normal. The music stops, leaving only a low clicking, buzzing, and humming sound. Lights shift.

Scene 4

The end of the day. Jessica reads to Erika from a manuscript.

JESSICA. "While it may be a useful exercise to question such things as organized religion, patriarchy, and antibiotics; in the end, we should acknowledge that Americans in the twenty-first century are, in the immortal words of Tina Turner, 'Simply the Best!' We have freedom, abundance, and most of all — " and this is in bold faced caps cuz it's also the title of her book " — WE CAN DO

WAY WAY MORE THAN THEY TELL US WE CAN!"

ERIKA. Where is she?

JESSICA. Meeting. She'll be back to give us the results.

ERIKA. When?

JESSICA. Soon! Listen to this —

ERIKA. Did she say you could read that?

JESSICA. She ASKED me to! This book'll be Oprah big. Listen — "Bill Clinton appointed more fat old women to more posts formerly held by fat old men than any president before him. He quietly altered the dynamics of gender in government, FOREVER. So he got serviced on the side. Big deal! Most wives would be relieved to be relieved of the duty!" Do you LOVE her?

ERIKA. Who do you think won the contest?

JESSICA. It's not a contest, it's an efficiency assessment.

ERIKA. It's a contest. There's gonna be a winner, and a whole bunch of losers.

JESSICA. Know what I heard Diana does? Pharmaceutical testosterone! THAT's where she gets the edge! I'm gonna try it!

ERIKA. Who told you that?

JESSICA. My phone friend at TTD.

ERIKA. You believe her?

JESSICA. She hears everything!

ERIKA. That doesn't make it true!

JESSICA. Jonathan's uncle is a former physician's assistant and he still has prescription pads. I'm totally trying it!

ERIKA. You don't just run out and try something like that! It could be dangerous! It could ruin your ... parts.

JESSICA. Erika, I really enjoy working with you. But you can be terribly naive.

ERIKA. I'm pregnant. *(Beat.)*

JESSICA. You are not!

ERIKA. I am.

JESSICA. You sure?

ERIKA. Yep.

JESSICA. Gyno?

ERIKA. Over-the-counter.

JESSICA. First Response?

ERIKA. EPT.

JESSICA. When?

ERIKA. Last night.

JESSICA. How far?

ERIKA. Four.

JESSICA. Months?

ERIKA. Weeks!

JESSICA. Whose? That Korean mid-level exec? *(Pause.)*

ERIKA. Remember when I had those marks on my leg? Those diamond-shaped imprints? Well remember how we ordered the floor mats for the exec suites and we opted for the premium plexiglass for added swivel-chair mobility? And they all have that diamond-shaped pattern pressed deep into their surface? *(Beat.)*

JESSICA. Xavier?

ERIKA. No. Solomon.

JESSICA. Eww! Solomon? You surrendered to an outright abuse of power?

ERIKA. No! I didn't surrender to anything. We were attracted to each other, and we became lovers. It's a relationship.

JESSICA. Bullshit!

ERIKA. I'm his mistress.

JESSICA. You're his homewrecking secretary.

ERIKA. You don't know what I am. You don't know goes on between us.

JESSICA. Yeah, and neither does his WIFE! And FAMILY!

ERIKA. His wife is nuts, OK? You should SEE the meds he has to get for her, the cocktails of anti-psychotics. She drives him insane! And this is a man who is already under a lot of pressure! And often in a great deal of pain! I massage his lower back and that is where he stores a lot of painful memories. He sometimes shares them with me. *(Beat. Jessica makes a disapproving sound.)* He's shares A LOT with me. You don't know. And sexually, he's a completely different person from the one you see in the well-cut suit, bossing people around. He's the opposite. He's actually really shy. It's so cute. The first time, he cried a little. I saw tears in his eyes. I'm telling you, the way he touches me — it's soft, and gentle. Even when we're only on the plexiglass floor mat. He's like a great big little boy. *(Beat.)* His car is huge and powerful, but it has this really quiet engine. Sometimes, afterwards, when he's driving me home, this phrase comes into my head over and over again — "luxury sedan." *(Beat.)* You wouldn't know what I'm talking about. *(Pause.)*

JESSICA. The first time I saw Jonathan, he has out smoking in the parking lot. He had one green Puma propped against the wall and he was leaning back all East of Eden-ish. He had on the dirtiest denim jacket, I mean stiff with filth. And he was doing this thing with his Zippo lighter. He was turning it over and over, just appreciating the smoothness of it in his hands. Without having to TALK about it, you know? Without having to turn to somebody else and go, "this is how it feels." The way, you know —

ERIKA. A girl would.

JESSICA. Yes. You know what I mean?

ERIKA. I do. *(Pause.)*

JESSICA. So Xavier never …

ERIKA. No.

JESSICA. So we just —

ERIKA. Yes.

JESSICA. And his wife has —

ERIKA. Terminal.

JESSICA. Man! *(Beat.)* What are you gonna do? I mean, just from a professional point of view I'd say a pregnancy would really slow you down around here.

ERIKA. I'm twice as fast a typist as you.

JESSICA. For now, but … with the bloating? Not to mention the stress.

ERIKA. God, this isn't the nineties.

JESSICA. What's that supposed to mean?

ERIKA. That I have options!

JESSICA. Oh my god. You're not stupid enough to think he's gonna leave his wife for you, are you? You don't think you have a future with him, do you? *(Beat.)*

ERIKA. You would never understand what we had.

JESSICA. Had? So it IS over. Oh, just as an FYI, you can see right through your shirt to your nipples. Diana told me to tell you that. If you're going to continue on the work track, you might want to invest in a decent blazer or a least a couple of opaque camisoles.

ERIKA. Um, so you and your girlfriend sit around and talk about my nipples? When are you starting a softball league?

JESSICA. You just don't have the maturity to understand a female model of mentorship.

ERIKA. I understand that you're jealous of me.

JESSICA. Oh yes, if only I could be a single, pregnant, semipermanent secretary!

ERIKA. You're semipermanent too!

JESSICA. I'm on my way up! *(Beat.)* Diana's got a couple more hours to do at her desk and she's sure to need food, so, would you mind ordering something up for her? I have information to prepare, so ...

ERIKA. I'm not getting her dinner! I'm not her wife.

JESSICA. Well. Why don't you go on home then. I've got a lot more work to do. *(Lights shift.)*

Scene 5

The break room. Next morning. Erika, Agatha, and Grace wait for Jessica.

GRACE. What are these?

AGATHA. They're fresh-baked strawberry cheesecake muffins and they're delicious. I made them for everybody.

GRACE. They look to die.

AGATHA. Erika, would you like one of my strawberry cheesecake muffins? Homemade?

ERIKA. If they're strawberry cheesecake, then by definition they are CUPCAKES, not MUFFINS.

AGATHA. The recipe says muffins.

GRACE. I brought in some fresh vegetables from our garden. We're two months ahead this year. They go on and on about global warming, but if it means sugar snap peas come sooner, how bad can it be?

AGATHA. I brought in some extra creamer. Not half-and-half. It's full heavy cream and it's delicious in coffee. I'll just put it right here for everyone to share. Erika?

ERIKA. I'm not hungry.

AGATHA. Just coffee?

ERIKA. I said I'm not HUNGRY!

AGATHA. But coffee is a beverage. *(A silence. Erika seethes.)*

GRACE. We're all a little pressured now, aren't we? Well it doesn't do us any good to fret. We'll get the results regardless.

AGATHA. That's right. *(They sit. Agatha takes out the heart.)* Why don't we just get started.

GRACE. What about Jessica?

AGATHA. She'll be in soon enough. It's our last heart talk before the efficiency verdict so I figure we might as well take all the time we can get! Can I remind everyone that this is for FEELINGS ONLY. No opinions. Just feelings. Would anyone like to get us started?

ERIKA. It's all your fault you know.

AGATHA. Erika, would you like the heart?

ERIKA. What exactly did you think you could accomplish? A purely professional environment? There's no such thing! A place to succeed on our own terms? Succeed at what? Bringing blueberry fucking cupcakes to the world?

AGATHA. Erika, I'm going to have to ask you to be quiet, as you do not have the heart! And I will remind you one last time that these are homemade, hand-mixed, strawberry cheesecake MUFFINS! *(Erika grabs the heart.)*

ERIKA. I'll tell you how I feel. I feel sick! *(Erika turns over the cupcakes, tosses the heart on the ground and runs out. Grace follows. Agatha kneels to pick up the pillow. Jessica walks in.)*

JESSICA. What did you do here? Jesus. What a mess. Where is everybody? *(Beat. Agatha doesn't answer, she holds the heart.)*

AGATHA. Excuse me, but I have the heart.

JESSICA. Oh, please. Are you gonna tell me what happened here?

AGATHA. I have one more thing to share, I'm ready.

JESSICA. *(Goes to Agatha, gestures to her to hand it over.)* Give it. Agatha. *(Jessica grabs the heart out of her hands. Agatha gasps.)*

AGATHA. That is not done.

JESSICA. I'm afraid I have something to share with you. You were all wrong about Xavier.

AGATHA. Why do you say that?

JESSICA. It was somebody else doing the harassing. It wasn't him.

AGATHA. Well of course.

JESSICA. You know that?

AGATHA. Well of course. I wrote those notes.

JESSICA. You lied?

AGATHA. I misled. But the truth was being told.

JESSICA. What about Xavier?

AGATHA. What about him? He got a luxurious severance package. He's better off for it.

JESSICA. No he didn't. He lost his severance package. And his wife has a uterus full of cancer! *(Beat.)*

AGATHA. I can't be fired for this. I have seniority. You don't even have your dental yet. I have head-to-toe health coverage, death and dismemberment benefits, and an almost fully vested retirement portfolio. *(Beat.)*

JESSICA. So it's true about you.

AGATHA. What's true about me?

JESSICA. That you hate men. That you're a man hater.

AGATHA. They say that?

JESSICA. Well I've heard it. *(Beat.)*

AGATHA. Let me tell you something — *(She stands, swoons.)* I think I'm having a hypoglycemic event. I need to eat something with a sugar content right now, or I don't know what I'll do. Where are my Nutter Butters when I need them?

JESSICA. I ate your Nutter Butters. *(A terrifying pause.)*

AGATHA. You what?

JESSICA. I ate your Nutter Butters with impunity. You shouldn't leave things hidden. It only heightens the incentive for hungry girls like me to take them.

AGATHA. My blood sugar just bottomed out. I'm dizzy. Can you please … *(She gestures that she wants the heart pillow, Jessica reluctantly hands it over.)* Thank you. *(She brightens up, sits as at a heart talk, starts to share.)* Well I'm sure you've all heard about it. I'm sure you have. So I've decided I'm ready to tell you myself.

JESSICA. Agatha, the heart talks are over. There's no one here!

AGATHA. They're not over yet! *(Beat. Jessica sits. Listens. Agatha continues.)* It was twenty years ago. Solomon gave me a project to help him present. He was going to use me in part of the presentation at Central, and we spent months planning it and putting it together. This was going to be my way out of the secretarial pool. Everyone thought I was nuts. They said as much. But I was under the impression that I might make a career for myself. And anyway, we were on our way into the conference room to have what would have been the first meeting of my new career and I tripped on a wedge of Laughing Cow cheese someone dropped from the hospitality tray, and fell flat on my face. My glasses broke and made a gash on my forehead. Hence, the bang. But that wasn't the worst of it. No, not even close. Solomon tipped his coffee over trying to stop my fall and it saturated my beautiful report, ruining the pie charts I'd hand-tinted — this was in the ditto days, mind you. But that wasn't the worst of it either. The worst of it was that my handbag opened up and everything in it spilled all over the conference room table. Maybelline pressed powder, half a pack of Rolos, a past-due phone bill. And an entire box of generic brand super-plus-size tampons emptied and scattered over the table, dropping in

people's coffee and expanding, rolling to a stop in front of the executives. All these men gathered from around the region, they were picking up the tampons and handing them to me. All I could do was take them, and say thank you, refill my purse of its contents, and sit in silence for the duration of the meeting. That was the end of my bid for upward mobility. I've stayed in clerical ever since. *(Pause. Jessica gets to her feet. Holds her head, a little dizzy.)*
JESSICA. I need to eat something too. There's vending machines in the janitorial break room. If we take the service elevator to the basement we can make it back in five for the meeting. I've got some change. *(Beat.)* We should hurry. Come on. *(Agatha moves to exit. Lights shift.)*

Scene 6

The ledge. Erika takes deep breaths, Grace is with her.

GRACE. I was exceptionally beautiful when I started working here. And I used it. I also knew it wouldn't last. A stolen weekend at the lake house is one thing, but a marriage is for good. *(Pause.)*
ERIKA. You and Solomon? *(Pause.)*
GRACE. It was a very long time ago.
ERIKA. When?
GRACE. It's been years.
ERIKA. How many years?
GRACE. My first year working as a secretary. That's what he likes. The first year. How long have you been here?
ERIKA. Eleven months. *(Long pause.)*
GRACE. You want to know the highlight of my work week? The absolute highlight of my work week is watering the potted plants in Solomon's office. I love the sound it makes when the water goes in. You can actually hear it being absorbed. It makes a kind of kissing sound. *(Beat.)* I've always found that the little things we do, the things that go unnoticed, these are what give us satisfaction. That's what your generation doesn't seem to get about being a woman. How far along are you?
ERIKA. How do you know?

GRACE. I know. I was too. How far along?

ERIKA. Just weeks.

GRACE. Have you decided?

ERIKA. No.

GRACE. We didn't have the choices you girls have today. Today you have a whole wealth of options. *(Erika lights a cigarette. Takes a long drag. Then another. Goes to drop it, takes one more, then drops it.)*

ERIKA. What did you do?

GRACE. I had the baby. I took medical leave. For six months, and then I gave it up for adoption. When you say it like that it sounds like you made an ATM deposit. Just dropped it in the slot. But it feels a little more like cutting your arm off at the elbow with a letter opener. It is the most painful thing you could imagine. *(Beat.)* But then I met Walter. And had Shelly. *(Beat.)*

ERIKA. And now ...

GRACE. Oh no, I'm not. I made that up. We were trying to find out if you were. *(Beat.)* We were just trying to make sure we did the right thing.

ERIKA. Did you?

GRACE. Oh yes. Marriage isn't easy. But it's right. *(Beat.)* You know something? I couldn't defecate with Walter in the house for the first six months of my marriage. Even if he was in the den with *60 Minutes* on full blast, I just couldn't do it. I had to wait until he left for work in the morning. Sometimes I sent him to the store for things I didn't really need. And as soon as the garage clicked shut I was fine. But until then ... well it was very uncomfortable. *(Beat.)* My mother, during the last years when Dad was so sick, she had to push suppositories into his body. She had to diaper him and wipe him. That's what it comes to, finally.

ERIKA. I know it's not emotional for him. I'm not a fucking IDIOT. He touches me like that because, because I just happen to have very soft skin. I've been ruthlessly exfoliating since my mother gave me my first loofah, at age eight. I know I'm just something that feels good to touch. I know that. *(Beat.)*

GRACE. You need to relax. The pressure is not good for the baby.

ERIKA. I didn't say I was having the baby.

GRACE. I know, I know. Let's get you off your feet. Why don't you go sit down. I'll bring you some herbal tea. You should be off coffee too. We need to go in and get the results. Come on now.

ERIKA. I know what I'm doing, okay?

GRACE. Of course you do. Do you have a supportive family?

ERIKA. I don't need to involve my family in this. I'm an adult.

GRACE. I was too. Honey, there's a terrible draft out here. Let's get you back inside and sit you down. Get you a cool drink of water. I've got peppermints in my purse.

ERIKA. Leave me alone! *(Beat.)* OK, I'm coming. I just need a minute. Please? I'll be back in a sec. I just need a moment by myself to think. *(Grace exits. Erika waits. Thinks. Lights shift.)*

Scene 7

Upbeat soft-rock office music builds to a deafening crescendo, then cuts out as lights bump up on Diana's door slamming shut. The office. Erika wears a blue ribbon lapel pin and faces out. The other three woman stand, stunned. A long, long pause.

JESSICA. Congrats.

ERIKA. Thanks. *(Jessica starts clearing off her desk.)*

JESSICA. Want my tape dispenser? I didn't order it from the catalogue. I bought it at this seaside boutique in Marin. They're real shells, see? One of them had a dead hermit crab in it at first so it started to smell. I had to crush it and push it out with a bobby pin. D'ju want it?

ERIKA. No, thanks. I don't like a lot of desk clutter.

JESSICA. I have about a thousand red Sharpies. I ordered way too many.

ERIKA. I don't need them.

JESSICA. Well they're not mine to take. So here you go. *(Dumps them on her desk. Agatha and Grace are still silent. Jessica turns to them.)* Does anyone want this tape dispenser? Guys? Hello? You could use this at home, couldn't you? For wrapping gifts and whatnot? I'll take my scissors, cuz those are useful. Can either of you use this? *(Pause.)*

GRACE. I'll take it. This year, I can wrap Walter's birthday gift at home instead of having them do it for me at the store. Thank you. This will be nice.

JESSICA. How about red Sharpies, do you have any need for red Sharpies? I have way too many of them. Will you need these at home? Agatha? A red permanent marker? For the road?

AGATHA. No thank you.

JESSICA. I thought her severance speech was a real cop-out. Totally derivative. Like we've never heard about "downsizing" before? I can't believe I was so into Diana! I don't know about you two, but I'm psyched to be redundant because now I can pursue my true interest. Hip-hop music. Listen to this. *(She puts on headphones. A rap.)*

   Think you can fuck with a bitch like me?
   Nigga PLEASE
   I'm the typa woman who could bring ya to yo knees
   I put you on hold
   Call you cold
   Open your mail
   And not break a nail
   Duplicate triplicate
   Bring it on
   I'm hip with it
   I'll staple you shut like Carni Wilson's belly
   Stop your attempt at talkin' like a militant Israeli
   I'll turn you over face down and fax you to Japan
   Then scan your ass digitally and do it all again

(She takes off her headphones.) I made it up. It's called Secretary Rap. I want to be the first rap artist with an exclusively clerical content. My name is gonna be White Out. Race-based puns ... VERY commercial. *(Beat.)* Jonathan said he'd help me record my shit. His stepdad gave him a full suite of studio-quality recording equipment when he graduated from rehab the first time. Isn't it a cool time to be alive? You can produce music from the privacy of your home, courtesy of the computer. Can you believe there was a time when electricity seemed like some kind of miracle, and now it's like, so what? So many things that seem impossible now are gonna be totally boring in just a few short years. It's so cool to think about. *(Beat.)* I heard that at Taylor, Traylor and Dane, they have unlimited free Snapple in the break room. I might pursue a part-time position there if my hip-hop doesn't blow up right away. Me and Jonathan really like Snapple. *(Erika starts to absorb her victory, Grace begins to clear her belongings, Jessica hums to herself as she loads up a box of belongings, Agatha sits, motionless. Lights shift.)*

Scene 8

The office. Months later. Erika sits at a cubicle, on a headset, visibly pregnant.

ERIKA. *SolomonSanbornSachs can I help you? Hello Diana. How was Vail? Yes everything's fine. Yes, I did. I was able to do that. Yes. Will do. Uh, Diana? I just had a question, I know we went over this at seminar but I have a question about the new break policy. I wanted to ask you if it's possible for us to take four fivers instead of two tenners. Because I would really prefer to have more of less, than less of more. (Beat.) Oh great, cuz, you know, I'm really starting to need those breaks. I mean my fiancé, Jai Sun, that's his whole name, Jai Sun, he's Korean, he wants me to stop working, but I don't think I need to stop until I have her. I just — (Beat.) No, no, I'm sorry. Yes of course. I understand. Of course. (Beat.) What? Oh, I said Korean. He's Korean. Koreans don't always dominate genetically. She could look like anyone in my family. We have strong strong genes. So ... (Beat.) No, they haven't told me that it's a girl. I can just tell. (Beat.) Yeah, I've heard that too. But I don't care if it's true or not. I choose to believe it. (Beat.) Of course, I'd be happy to, what would you like today? Uh-huh. Are you sure you don't want to try the Caribbean Tuna Salad? It's a little lighter than the Chicken Caesar and every bit as satisfying. OK, I'll order it now and it'll be on your desk when you get back. Anything else you need? Uh-huh. Of course. No problem. Well, if you think of anything else, I'll be here. That's my job. (Lights fade.)*

End of Play

PROPERTY LIST

Cubicle decorations: dried flowers, photos, beanie babies
Telephones
Computers
Heart-shaped pillow (ERIKA, AGATHA)
Paper cups of coffee (JESSICA, ERIKA)
Mugs of coffee (GRACE, AGATHA)
Steno pad (AGATHA)
Pencil (AGATHA)
Note cards (JESSICA)
Headsets (JESSICA, ERIKA, GRACE, AGATHA)
Typewriter (AGATHA)
Correction tape (AGATHA)
Memos (AGATHA, JESSICA)
Purse (GRACE)
Cigarettes (ERIKA, GRACE)
Lighter (GRACE)
Sweet'N Low (AGATHA)
Spoon (AGATHA)
Photo (AGATHA)
Watch (GRACE)
Mini-refrigerator (JESSICA)
Tupperware container of non-dairy creamer (JESSICA)
Cell phone (ERIKA)
Pager (ERIKA)
Pretzels (JESSICA)
Nutter Butters (JESSICA)
Compact (JESSICA)
Lip gloss (JESSICA)
Papers (ERIKA)
Labeler (JESSICA)
Trash can (ERIKA)
Altoids tin (ERIKA)
Half-and-half (AGATHA)
Manuscript (JESSICA)
Box (JESSICA)

SOUND EFFECTS

Phones ringing
Computers beeping
Alarm blasts
Wind, street noise
Traffic sounds
Pager beeping
Street sounds, honking, etc.

NEW PLAYS

★ **MONTHS ON END by Craig Pospisil.** In comic scenes, one for each month of the year, we follow the intertwined worlds of a circle of friends and family whose lives are poised between happiness and heartbreak. "...a triumph...these twelve vignettes all form crucial pieces in the eternal puzzle known as human relationships, an area in which the playwright displays an assured knowledge that spans deep sorrow to unbounded happiness." *–Ann Arbor News.* "...rings with emotional truth, humor...[an] endearing contemplation on love...entertaining and satisfying." *–Oakland Press.* [5M, 5W] ISBN: 0-8222-1892-5

★ **GOOD THING by Jessica Goldberg.** Brings us into the households of John and Nancy Roy, forty-something high-school guidance counselors whose marriage has been increasingly on the rocks and Dean and Mary, recent graduates struggling to make their way in life. "...a blend of gritty social drama, poetic humor and unsubtle existential contemplation..." *–Variety.* [3M, 3W] ISBN: 0-8222-1869-0

★ **THE DEAD EYE BOY by Angus MacLachlan.** Having fallen in love at their Narcotics Anonymous meeting, Billy and Shirley-Diane are striving to overcome the past together. But their relationship is complicated by the presence of Sorin, Shirley-Diane's fourteen-year-old son, a damaged reminder of her dark past. "...a grim, insightful portrait of an unmoored family..." *–NY Times.* "MacLachlan's play isn't for the squeamish, but then, tragic stories delivered at such an unrelenting fever pitch rarely are." *–Variety.* [1M, 1W, 1 boy] ISBN: 0-8222-1844-5

★ **[SIC] by Melissa James Gibson.** In adjacent apartments three young, ambitious neighbors come together to discuss, flirt, argue, share their dreams and plan their futures with unequal degrees of deep hopefulness and abject despair. "A work...concerned with the sound and power of language..." *–NY Times.* "...a wonderfully original take on urban friendship and the comedy of manners—a *Design for Living* for our times..." *–NY Observer.* [3M, 2W] ISBN: 0-8222-1872-0

★ **LOOKING FOR NORMAL by Jane Anderson.** Roy and Irma's twenty-five-year marriage is thrown into turmoil when Roy confesses that he is actually a woman trapped in a man's body, forcing the couple to wrestle with the meaning of their marriage and the delicate dynamics of family. "Jane Anderson's bittersweet transgender domestic comedy-drama ...is thoughtful and touching and full of wit and wisdom. A real audience pleaser." *–Hollywood Reporter.* [5M, 4W] ISBN: 0-8222-1857-7

★ **ENDPAPERS by Thomas McCormack.** The regal Joshua Maynard, the old and ailing head of a mid-sized, family-owned book-publishing house in New York City, must name a successor. One faction in the house backs a smart, "pragmatic" manager, the other faction a smart, "sensitive" editor and both factions fear what the other's man could do to this house— and to them. "If Kaufman and Hart had undertaken a comedy about the publishing business, they might have written *Endpapers*...a breathlessly fast, funny, and thoughtful comedy ...keeps you amused, guessing, and often surprised...profound in its empathy for the paradoxes of human nature." *–NY Magazine.* [7M, 4W] ISBN: 0-8222-1908-5

★ **THE PAVILION by Craig Wright.** By turns poetic and comic, romantic and philosophical, this play asks old lovers to face the consequences of difficult choices made long ago. "The script's greatest strength lies in the genuineness of its feeling." *–Houston Chronicle.* "Wright's perceptive, gently witty writing makes this familiar situation fresh and thoroughly involving." *–Philadelphia Inquirer.* [2M, 1W (flexible casting)] ISBN: 0-8222-1898-4

DRAMATISTS PLAY SERVICE, INC.
440 Park Avenue South, New York, NY 10016 212-683-8960 Fax 212-213-1539
postmaster@dramatists.com www.dramatists.com

NEW PLAYS

★ **BE AGGRESSIVE by Annie Weisman.** Vista Del Sol is paradise, sandy beaches, avocado-lined streets. But for seventeen-year-old cheerleader Laura, everything changes when her mother is killed in a car crash, and she embarks on a journey to the Spirit Institute of the South where she can learn "cheer" with Bible belt intensity. "...filled with lingual gymnastics...stylized rapid-fire dialogue..." –*Variety*. "...a new, exciting, and unique voice in the American theatre..." –*BackStage West*. [1M, 4W, extras] ISBN: 0-8222-1894-1

★ **FOUR by Christopher Shinn.** Four people struggle desperately to connect in this quiet, sophisticated, moving drama. "...smart, broken-hearted...Mr. Shinn has a precocious and forgiving sense of how power shifts in the game of sexual pursuit...He promises to be a playwright to reckon with..." –*NY Times*. "A voice emerges from an American place. It's got humor, sadness and a fresh and touching rhythm that tell of the loneliness and secrets of life...[a] poetic, haunting play." –*NY Post*. [3M, 1W] ISBN: 0-8222-1850-X

★ **WONDER OF THE WORLD by David Lindsay-Abaire.** A madcap picaresque involving Niagara Falls, a lonely tour-boat captain, a pair of bickering private detectives and a husband's dirty little secret. "Exceedingly whimsical and playfully wicked. Winning and genial. A top-drawer production." –*NY Times*. "Full frontal lunacy is on display. A most assuredly fresh and hilarious tragicomedy of marital discord run amok...absolutely hysterical..." –*Variety*. [3M, 4W (doubling)] ISBN: 0-8222-1863-1

★ **QED by Peter Parnell.** Nobel Prize-winning physicist and all-around genius Richard Feynman holds forth with captivating wit and wisdom in this fascinating biographical play that originally starred Alan Alda. "QED is a seductive mix of science, human affections, moral courage, and comic eccentricity. It reflects on, among other things, death, the absence of God, travel to an unexplored country, the pleasures of drumming, and the need to know and understand." –*NY Magazine*. "Its rhythms correspond to the way that people—even geniuses—approach and avoid highly emotional issues, and it portrays Feynman with affection and awe." –*The New Yorker*. [1M, 1W] ISBN: 0-8222-1924-7

★ **UNWRAP YOUR CANDY by Doug Wright.** Alternately chilling and hilarious, this deliciously macabre collection of four bedtime tales for adults is guaranteed to keep you awake for nights on end. "Engaging and intellectually satisfying...a treat to watch." –*NY Times*. "Fiendishly clever. Mordantly funny and chilling. Doug Wright teases, freezes and zaps us." –*Village Voice*. "Four bite-size plays that bite back." –*Variety*. [flexible casting] ISBN: 0-8222-1871-2

★ **FURTHER THAN THE FURTHEST THING by Zinnie Harris.** On a remote island in the middle of the Atlantic secrets are buried. When the outside world comes calling, the islanders find their world blown apart from the inside as well as beyond. "Harris winningly produces an intimate and poetic, as well as political, family saga." –*Independent (London)*. "Harris' enthralling adventure of a play marks a departure from stale, well-furrowed theatrical terrain." –*Evening Standard (London)*. [3M, 2W] ISBN: 0-8222-1874-7

★ **THE DESIGNATED MOURNER by Wallace Shawn.** The story of three people living in a country where what sort of books people like to read and how they choose to amuse themselves becomes both firmly personal and unexpectedly entangled with questions of survival. "This is a playwright who does not just tell you what it is like to be arrested at night by goons or to fall morally apart and become an aimless yet weirdly contented ghost yourself. He has the originality to make you feel it." –*Times (London)*. "A fascinating play with beautiful passages of writing..." –*Variety*. [2M, 1W] ISBN: 0-8222-1848-8

DRAMATISTS PLAY SERVICE, INC.
440 Park Avenue South, New York, NY 10016 212-683-8960 Fax 212-213-1539
postmaster@dramatists.com   www.dramatists.com

NEW PLAYS

★ **SHEL'S SHORTS by Shel Silverstein.** Lauded poet, songwriter and author of children's books, the incomparable Shel Silverstein's short plays are deeply infused with the same wicked sense of humor that made him famous. "…[a] childlike honesty and twisted sense of humor." *—Boston Herald.* "…terse dialogue and an absurdity laced with a tang of dread give [*Shel's Shorts*] more than a trace of Samuel Beckett's comic existentialism." *—Boston Phoenix.* [flexible casting] ISBN: 0-8222-1897-6

★ **AN ADULT EVENING OF SHEL SILVERSTEIN by Shel Silverstein.** Welcome to the darkly comic world of Shel Silverstein, a world where nothing is as it seems and where the most innocent conversation can turn menacing in an instant. These ten imaginative plays vary widely in content, but the style is unmistakable. "…[*An Adult Evening*] shows off Silverstein's virtuosic gift for wordplay…[and] sends the audience out…with a clear appreciation of human nature as perverse and laughable." *—NY Times.* [flexible casting] ISBN: 0-8222-1873-9

★ **WHERE'S MY MONEY? by John Patrick Shanley.** A caustic and sardonic vivisection of the institution of marriage, laced with the author's inimitable razor-sharp wit. "…Shanley's gift for acid-laced one-liners and emotionally tumescent exchanges is certainly potent…" *—Variety.* "…lively, smart, occasionally scary and rich in reverse wisdom." *—NY Times.* [3M, 3W] ISBN: 0-8222-1865-8

★ **A FEW STOUT INDIVIDUALS by John Guare.** A wonderfully screwy comedy-drama that figures Ulysses S. Grant in the throes of writing his memoirs, surrounded by a cast of fantastical characters, including the Emperor and Empress of Japan, the opera star Adelina Patti and Mark Twain. "Guare's smarts, passion and creativity skyrocket to awesome heights…" *—Star Ledger.* "…precisely the kind of good new play that you might call an everyday miracle…every minute of it is fresh and newly alive…" *—Village Voice.* [10M, 3W] ISBN: 0-8222-1907-7

★ **BREATH, BOOM by Kia Corthron.** A look at fourteen years in the life of Prix, a Bronx native, from her ruthless girl-gang leadership at sixteen through her coming to maturity at thirty. "…vivid world, believable and eye-opening, a place worthy of a dramatic visit, where no one would want to live but many have to." *—NY Times.* "…rich with humor, terse vernacular strength and gritty detail…" *—Variety.* [1M, 9W] ISBN: 0-8222-1849-6

★ **THE LATE HENRY MOSS by Sam Shepard.** Two antagonistic brothers, Ray and Earl, are brought together after their father, Henry Moss, is found dead in his seedy New Mexico home in this classic Shepard tale. "…His singular gift has been for building mysteries out of the ordinary ingredients of American family life…" *—NY Times.* "…rich moments …Shepard finds gold." *—LA Times.* [7M, 1W] ISBN: 0-8222-1858-5

★ **THE CARPETBAGGER'S CHILDREN by Horton Foote.** One family's history spanning from the Civil War to WWII is recounted by three sisters in evocative, intertwining monologues. "…bittersweet music—[a] rhapsody of ambivalence…in its modest, garrulous way…theatrically daring." *—The New Yorker.* [3W] ISBN: 0-8222-1843-7

★ **THE NINA VARIATIONS by Steven Dietz.** In this funny, fierce and heartbreaking homage to *The Seagull*, Dietz puts Chekhov's star-crossed lovers in a room and doesn't let them out. "A perfect little jewel of a play…" *—Shepherdstown Chronicle.* "…a delightful revelation of a writer at play; and also an odd, haunting, moving theater piece of lingering beauty." *—Eastside Journal (Seattle).* [1M, 1W (flexible casting)] ISBN: 0-8222-1891-7

DRAMATISTS PLAY SERVICE, INC.
440 Park Avenue South, New York, NY 10016 212-683-8960 Fax 212-213-1539
postmaster@dramatists.com www.dramatists.com